SWIMMING, NOT DROWNING

Poems

Mari-Carmen Marín

Legacy Book Press LLC
Camanche, Iowa

He was having a dialogue with Sonny. He wanted Sonny to leave the shoreline and strike out for the deep water. He was Sonny's witness that deep water and drowning were not the same thing—he had been there, and he knew. And he wanted Sonny to know. He was waiting for Sonny to do the things on the keys which would let Creole know that Sonny was in the water.

~James Baldwin's "Sonny's Blues"

for my mom and all those who suffer from mental illness.
You are not alone.

TABLE OF CONTENTS

Acknowledgements

Thanks to the editors of the following publications in which some of my poems, sometimes in earlier forms, first appeared:

- *Scarlet Leaf Review*: "A Seven-Year-Old Wonders," and "The Naked Child."
- *The Awakenings Review*: "The First Time It Happened," "It's All in Your Head," "In Answer to Those Who Say the Voices in My Head Are Not Real," "The Soul Killer," and "The Fall."
- *Lucky Jefferson*: "In the Therapist's Chair."
- *The Green Light Literary Journal*: "Weeds."
- *The Comstock Review*: "Cast Away," and "Fuguilla."
- *Breath & Shadow Magazine*: "When You Stop Caring."
- *The Poetic Bond X*: "Blame It on the Rum and Coke," and "Who Can Answer?"
- *Keleidoscope: Exploring the Experience of Disability through Literature and the Fine Arts*: "Intruders," "When You Stop Caring," and "How to Tame Wild Thoughts."

~ ~ ~

I would like to begin by expressing my gratitude to Lone Star College—Tomball, for granting me a sabbatical leave for the 2020 spring semester. Without this time off from teaching, I would have been unable to work on finishing this book, which was cooking up for years.

I would also like to thank my students, who have taught me to be present and listen. Along the years, I have had the pleasurable but difficult job of being one of the people they could trust to open up and talk about their mental health issues. By sharing my own struggles, I have let them know they are not alone, and I have not felt alone. By validating their experiences, I have also validated my own.

I could not be more thankful for the poets who have taught me the nuts and bolts of writing poetry and introduced me to writers whose work has inspired me for years, poets like Dave Parsons, Tony Hoagland, Beth Lyons, Mong-Lan, Kirsten Andersen, and Courtney Kampa. I want to thank them for their time, knowledge, expertise, passion, and careful feedback during workshops.

Special gratitude goes to my psychologists at different times in my life: María Dolores Baena Sánchez, Becky Stidham, and Douglas Chan, without whose empathetic listening, advice, and lessons, I would have sunk in the waters of depression and drowned.

I'm very grateful to my dear friend, colleague, and poet, Catherine C. Olson, who is always willing to read my poems, offer feedback, and support me during both good and bad times. Katie, your loyalty, compassion, and steady heart keep me going.

I want to thank my dad for his example, for always believing in me, and for imbuing a life-long love for learning and the arts in me. I also want to thank my sister and brother for always standing by my side and picking me up when I fall; and of course, many thanks need to go to my mom, whose hard work, sacrifices, and strength in the face of adversity have taught me the real meaning and power of selfless love.

Finally, this book would not have come into being without the support and love of my husband, Paul, the patient mender capable of putting all the pieces back together when I break, and my son, Jackson, who brought new meaning to my life the moment he was born. You two are the pillars that hold me strong and stop me from falling apart.

Cover Artwork Statement

Marcela Bolívar is a Brazilian-born Colombian artist based in Germany. She works as an illustrator for various international publishing houses while developing further her personal work. Her images aim to disengage photomontage of its technologic and automated nature, pushing the technical limits of photography and digital media as they are merged with a variety of pictorial expressions. The mixture of diverse media such as painting, photo, 3d elements and sculpture brings forth a personal interpretation of the world that lingers between reality and fiction, disguise and truth.

Being underwater has always fascinated me. As humans, we are so unwelcome in this element, everything is against us; our bodies try their best to survive. I was really inspired by the atmosphere and spirit Mari Carmen described to me based on her poetry. This body in particular stands against the elements and thrives after feeling everything was lost. These images show not only the struggle of a person to live, but a new place where she finally finds herself.

Preface

Since the age of thirteen, I have suffered from anxiety and depression, two mental health issues that affect more than 264 million of people of all ages worldwide ("Depression")[1].

However, I was not officially diagnosed with these disorders or treated until I turned twenty-three in the mid nineteen-nineties, and even then, depression and anxiety were misunderstood and dismissed as something a person could snap out with words of encouragement and some good reasoning. It is twenty something years later, and there are still many misconceptions and shame surrounding these two and other very real and serious mental disorders.

This book is about the storms that strike us, making us fall into the rough waters, where we think we'll drown, until with much practice, understanding, and support, we learn how to not only keep our heads above water, but also swim back to the shore. This book is about not giving up, about becoming what James Baldwin described in his story "Sonny's Blues" as "witness[es] that deep water and drowning [are] not the same thing."

---

[1] Depression can also lead to suicide, and suicide is the "second leading cause of death in 15-29-year-olds." "Depression." *World Health Organization (WHO)*, 30 Jan. 2020, https://www.who.int/news-room/fact-sheets/detail/depression. Accessed 19 Feb. 2020.

I am hoping to raise awareness and offer hope to those who suffer in silence from mental illness, through the powerful art of poetry. Like music and any other forms of art, poetry has the power to look past differences by reflecting on what makes us all part of the same universe, the power to open doors where there were barriers, the power to transcend limits and remind us that we, too, can be Robert Frost's swinger of birches. Poetry elevates our souls. Poetry heals. Poetry inspires.

I
DEEP WATERS

"Stories Chase and Bite and Hunt"[2]

Some stories are sweet:
    One summer night when I was four,
    I went running to my room—pressed
    palms against my chest, eyes closed,
    head bowed—and asked the Virgin Mary
    on the wall to erase mom's frown and paint
    a smile as bright and broad as the circus
    clowns' whose songs I used to play
    when I was sick in bed for days.

Some stories are fun:
    Later the same year—it was the end
    of fall—I sneaked into mom's room
    and took to school her fancy embroidered
    handkerchiefs—to offer them to other
    girls, who promised me to be best friends
    and play together in return.

But other stories leave deep scars:
    Málaga, 1978,
    my parents' bedroom,
    cloudy Sunday morning,
    a timid sun peeking through the curtains.
    Dad's sitting in a rocking chair.
    Mom's braiding my sister's hair.

---

[2] Quote from Patrick Ness's novel, *A Monster Calls*. Candlewick Press, 2011, p. 35.

I'm standing at the door.
Can't remember why.
Can't remember much,
but my mother's biting words:

> "If your dad and I ever get divorced,
> I will keep your sister;
> your dad will keep you."

A Seven-Year-Old Wonders

Mami, is abuelo in heaven with Diosito? *Sure he is.*
abuelo era un santo. Does he see us from there? *He sees*
us all and prays for us. Did he take his glasses with him?
The round little ones he's wearing in the picture next
to abuela's? *In heaven, he doesn't need glasses.* You mean
Diosito is an eye doctor? *Diosito is more than a doctor.*
He's todo-poderoso. You mean like Superman? *He's more*
poderoso than Superman. So, if abuelo can see us, is he
sad when you cry and stop talking to papi? Uh… I
guess he is. I don't know, mi niña.

Mami, is heaven a city above the clouds? *I don't think*
so. So, what does heaven look like? *I don't know.*
Nobody knows. So why do people look up to the sky
when they talk about heaven? *I guess it's invisible, like*
air, like Diosito. Is that why abuelo doesn't need glasses
to see you, because he's invisible? *In heaven, people are*
perfect. There's no need for glasses, doctors, or pain. So he
doesn't feel sad when you cry and stop talking to
papi? *Uh… I guess he does, but in a different way. I don't*
know, mi niña.

Mami, will you go to heaven when you die? *I hope so. I*
don't know. Why don't you know? *Maybe I'm not good*
enough. Is that why you cry and stop talking to papi?
No! Well… Maybe. I don't know, mi niña. So mami, if
you go to heaven—and I want you to go—will I find
you when I die? *Uh… I don't know. I hope so. There is*

nothing to worry about, cielo. We will all be with Diosito. But why can't I be with you, too? I'll feel lost. I'll be scared… and how will I know if you stopped crying and being silent for days?

Behind Walls

On Sundays, Mom's silence claims
its space between the ceiling, floor,
and four walls of every room, enshrouding
the house with a smothering cloak
of unanswered questions:

What did I do? Is it something I said?
Maybe I didn't do what I said I would.
Why are Mom's eyes iron-clad? Why
are her fists like tightly closed clams?

Mom's silence lingers on, heavy with voices unwilling
       to speak:

the voice of a bird shrieking her pain after falling,
of a fugitive slave unknowing of the path to her
       freedom,
of a child screaming her frustration at her parents,

the voice of a sculptor trying to mold hard pieces of
       clay,
of the clay that can't be molded after hardening.
of the proud wounded soldier bleeding to her death.

Who dares to invoke voices as deafening
as mom's Sundays' silence?

Not me. I'm scared, or maybe too young
to do so. Instead, I call on the voices of
Christie's Poirot and Blyton's Famous Five
to talk to me and help me survive
another loud silent Sunday.

The First Time It Happened

I remember the tingling in my fingers—
an ant trail down to the tips.
I remember my thumbs bending
and locking in place
in rigor mortis,
only I was alive,
a twelve-year-old girl
standing outside
my math classroom
in Madre de la Luz Middle School,
"Mother of Light,"
and yet
I felt motherless,
trapped in a dark place
I did not recognize.

I remember my lungs
shrinking—
I wanted to breathe
long deep breaths,
as if getting ready
to dive in the sea
where we went to swim
on San Miguel beach
every summer.
I remember inhaling,
the air caught
in my throat.

I remember my heart
jumping in my chest,
trying to warn me
I needed to breathe.

I remember shaking like
a child with a febrile seizure,
and then,
sobbing
deep racking sobs,

all happening
in an eternal minute
before a test,

all happening
in front of a crowd
of students I was
careful to impress

until my teacher,
Don Miguel Pelayo,
came out and hugged me,
his arms like a blanket
covering a survivor
of a shipwreck,
his soothing voice
whispering, "It's okay;
you are okay."

It's All in Your Head

The first night, I dream of
being stranded in the ocean,
no ship, no land, no people.
Giant waves drag me down.
I sink; then rise; I sink again; I
can't move my legs. I'm drowning . . .
Then, I'm sitting up on my bed coughing,
gasping for air—my sister's steady breathing
brings me to reality. It's 4 a.m.; it's calm;
I'm home; I'm dry; I'm alive.

The second night I fall asleep easily
only to wake up five hours later
panting, crying, sweating.
I go to the bathroom to grab a tissue.
The girl in the mirror looks pale;
strands of her long hair stick to her cheeks and neck.
I look at her, wash and dry her face until some color
returns to her skin and she looks calmer.
Back in bed, I pray for the morning to arrive fast.

The third night I don't want to fall asleep.
What if I forget to breathe and don't wake up?
What if I die? I'm too young, three days before I turn sixteen.
Fear kidnaps my nerves,
ties them with electric wire.

Daylight is my lifesaver, but not today,
Sunday, a sunny and breezy winter day.
I step out of the house and the door slams
behind me, sucking up the air I need to breathe.
I bend over to get my breath back,
and that's it.
I've had enough.

Sitting in a cold room of the Torrecárdenas
    Hospital—
my dad's arm around my shoulder, my mom's legs
crossing and uncrossing, crossing and uncrossing—
I remember the time I asked Mom whether families
reconnected in heaven. "Don't know," she answered.

When Dr. Pardo enters the room—my X-rays in his
    right hand—
he examines my chest, smiles and says,
"You are fine.
Take Valium for three nights.
It's all in your head."

Wounded

The vipers you spit
sink their fangs into my chest. I
bleed tears of venom.

Weird – Part I

"A broken bone can heal, but the wound
a word opens can fester forever"
~Jessamyn West

You sit at the back of the classroom,
black hoodie, tight pants, knee-high
buckled-up boots, thick eyeliner shaded
eyes that seek to be noticed but unjudged.

Weird.

You choose broccoli over fries,
don't eat meat, or fish, or dairy,
and chocolate makes you gag.

Weird.

You stay home during weekends, watching
music videos on *MTV*, dancing in front of
your mirrored closet doors, perfecting those
Michael Jackson's "Beat It" moves, and reading
young adult novels of friendships and first loves.

Weird.

You cringe at the thought of a room
full of strangers, where you're supposed
to mingle, and talk, and laugh. The room
becomes a prison, and you just want to run.

Weird.

Resulting syllogism:

If being different means being weird,
and being weird means being wrong,
then, being different means being wrong,
and you are different, weird, and wrong,
wrong,
wrong.

Loving You Is Like . . .

walking a tightrope,
the wire cutting my bare feet.
You push me; I fall.

Blame It on the Rum and Coke

I saw him in church every Sunday—a Spanish version
of a *Risky Business* Tom Cruise—sitting in the front
     pew
on the left aisle with his family. Once, I caught him
     looking

at me. Eighteen and my heart had not beaten so fast
     before.
Glances were exchanged during months. I was Julie
     Delpy
stealing looks at Ethan Hawke in the cabin of a
     Vienna Park

Ferris Wheel. One night in June, he was at my best
     friend's
birthday party, a mirage in the suddenly hot room
     where he sat
next to me. We talked all night long. I learned he liked
     Michael

Bolton, Rubén Darío's poems, bonfires on the beach,
     and drinking
rum and coke until dawn. A few weeks later he kissed
     me on my lips,
taking the breath I was holding for so long. When
     asked to be his

girlfriend, I thought I was living in a dream . . .

until it became a nightmare:

Summer break.   He left for San José.
        Saw him twice.   Acted like strangers.
    Third time we saw each other
            in la Feria de Almería   he got drunk
    —rum and coke, and rum and coke, and—
    disappeared.   Found him wasted
                making out with a girl,
        a friend of his I'd never met.   I left,
    a dagger in my back.   Following day he
claimed nothing had happened.
                "Choose, her or me?"
He chose her.   We parted ways.
                Never saw him again.

The Masquerade

When you don't see what you want to see,
you see what I want you to see.
But you never see Me. I hide behind
the mask, the mask you help decorate with
parts of your personal history through threats
of inadequacy and rejection and
promises of approval.

The mask I wear to chameleon
my way through each day, with which
I perform, perfect, please, and prove
that I am worthy of your love.

The mask I take off at night, exposing
an alien woman desperate to breathe,
the mask without which I feel

naked and flawed, but also
light, authentic, and free.

When the Road to Perfection Leads to Perdition

You give me roses.
The thorns tear into my flesh,
blood oozes through my fingers,
and tears blur my vision.

You give me water.
I drown in the spring,
and I am left unsated,
fighting off the thought
of waterfalls cascading
                          down
                                  my throat.

You take my hand.
I can't keep your pace.
                              I fall.
I gasp for air,
but no air seems enough
                                 and you leave,
without me.

Quarter-Life Crisis

<u>Plymouth, August 1996</u>
Relentless rain;
only one small window in my attic room;
cold winds cut my face, pierce my clothes;
five p.m. nights, five a.m. mornings;
a sunless sky in mourning;
waiting for a bus on the wrong side of the road;
guys preying on my foreignness, wanting to save me
from loneliness by taking me on pub tours, covering
    my shoulders
with their coats, touching my knees with their knees
under tea-room tables, stroking my hair in their cars
as they whisper, "I can make you happy."
But I shy away, a puppy
surrounded by a pack of wolves.
Two weeks, and I leave for home.

<u>Almería, September 1996</u>
The list of mistakes I made this past year pile up in
    my mind like cars
crashing against each other on a foggy night: applying
    for the Teaching
Abroad Program without a second thought; believing
    he would come
with me; letting him play the now-I-see-you-now-I-
    don't
game, even if it hurt; agreeing to a year in England,
    though I did not want

to go; convincing myself I could do it even if I knew I
    could not.

Twenty-three, a bachelor's degree my greatest
    achievement, tainted
by my rushed return from Plymouth. Now I feel like a
    stray dog, head
and ears down, tail tucked between my legs, lost on
    the side of a road
to nowhere, sulking.

"Prozac is the god of emotional numbness,"
claimed Don Luis, my mother's psychiatrist.
It must be true. I lean toward the mirror, blue
eyeliner for my eyes, blue

mascara for my lashes, the blue
calmness of the cloudless sky hiding
the real storm raging inside me. Four
days ago, I was spinning out of control,

riding down the waterfalls of my emotions. Today,
I can float on the stream after the fall. I take up my
briefcase and head to my first day of work, tutoring
a student at her home. Behind me I hear the roaring

waters against the rocks. I walk on.

Conflict

Dense fog enshrouds you
in a cold veil. You can't see
the smile in his eyes.

Cast Away

"I want a divorce."

Three rooms and four walls
could not stop the tsunami of
my father's words. Giant waves
echoed throughout my adult body
and my lungs began to squeeze
until my breaths _ became _ short.

No sturdy dam could have protected
me from the ice in his voice and the mud
in my mother's plea for a second chance.

Not twenty-seven years of intensive learning—
learning to sail the ocean of silence
separating my two harbors,
learning how to anchor
to my father's evenings in the dining-room,
        getting lost in Dostoyevsky's Russia
        with the help of Mozart's symphonies,
while my mother watched TV in the living-room
to quiet the demons in her mind, after long days
of teaching, cooking, cleaning . . .
making sure everybody else's needs were met
but her own.

Nor could the life vest of adulthood
help me swim through the turbulent waters
that flooded my two harbors.

Four months later, my father was gone,
and I floated, trying to grasp any
valuable remains of the wreckage.

When the Blindfold Falls

I was naïve to think love meant
your hand-written sonnets
in lined scratch paper
sneaked between the pages
of my computer notes.

> I was naïve to think love meant
> us on a secluded bench on the far side
> of the San José beach walk,
> breathing the salty breeze—
> your chest my pillow,
> my hair your harp,
> at four a.m.

I was naïve to think love meant
Four—sometimes more—
phone calls a day –for three years straight—
with your whispered *te amo*'s,
mi amiga del alma.

> I was naïve to think love meant
> twenty-five roses
> for the twenty-five years
> (five less than yours)
> *that I'd enriched the earth*
> *on which I stood*—You claimed.

And yet,

You were naïve to think
love could just live
on poetry, roses, phone calls,
on dreamy nights contemplating the sea,
and nothing else.

"It Is Better to Be Alive Than Better"[3]

"So let's try Zyprexa."

I nod at his words. What do I know about
    antidepressants? I
just want to feel better, no more crying spells after
    knocking
down a glass on the coffee table with my elbow, its
    broken
shards scattered across the floor like fragments of my
    shattered
mind, no more restless nights of screams, air punches
    and kicks,
no more empty minutes staring at the wall looking for
    cracks and
holes, wondering where they would take me if I was
    an ant, wanting
to be an ant and not a woman in her thirties who
    can't be happy. Maybe
Marcellus Emants was right when he said that only a
    fool can be happy.
Does that mean I'm not a fool? Does that mean I am
    smart? Then, being
smart is not as good as I thought, or is it? I'm
    confused!
The doctor knows better,

---

[3] Zucker, Rachel. *Museum of Accidents*, Wave Books, 2009 (p. 24).

I want to believe. And one week later, I am better, no
    nightmares or
hysterical crying, no desire to be an ant inside wall
    holes and cracks,
no drama, no-thing. This must be what robots feel, or
    rather, not
feel, just movement, doing this, doing that, and more
doing after this and that.

  ((It is Monday, September 19, 2005. School will
  be canceled during the rest of the week. A girl in
  my second-grade class is crying at dismissal time.
  Sandra worries that Hurricane Rita will bring down
  her house and everything inside. I give her a hug
  and dry her tears with my hands. "It will be okay,"
  I tell her, and to my surprise, I mean it))

This category 5 monster does not scare me!

The following day, all morning long,
the phone does not stop
ringing. "Are you leaving
Houston?" "Why not?" "It is very dangerous!"
"Forget about the cats!" "You're going to give
me a heart attack!" "What's wrong with you?"
"Leave before it's too late!" "I won't sleep
until you leave." My parents' concern hits
a closed door that Zyprexa refuses to open.
The news in Spain always blows things out
of proportion! That must be it.

((Paul boards all the windows of our rented
tree house and piles sandbags at the bottom
of the front and back doors; he moves all the plants
inside our living-room, a temporary greenhouse))

So glad my name is not Rita!
That night I sleep like a child on Benadryl.

"Wake up! We're leaving!" Paul has already
packed two small suitcases with clothes and
some valuables. The cats are in their crates,
not without complaining. "We're going to
my aunt's at Bellville," he says. "We'll be
safe there. And please call your parents." I
do as I'm told, no questions asked, no thoughts
of leaving everything I own behind, no worries
about losing my present and future.

((Horrific traffic jams; people driving on the wrong
side of the roads; overheated cars; cars running out
of gas; honking; cursing; one-hundred degrees
Fahrenheit; a meow competition between Chiqui
and Eddie; a ninety-minute trip made in ten hours))

The cats run and hide under the skirt of a table
in the back room of Paul's aunt's house at Bellville,
finally released from their cages but now in alien
territory. We go to bed early. "How are you feeling?"
Paul asks me. "I'm fine," and I mean it.

In the darkness of the room,
I run through a list of things
that have happened in the last
three days. *What's wrong with
me?* I try to open the door Zyprexa
closed to no avail. *Am I really better?*

Maybe it's better to be alive than better.

Death

A merciless thief,
preying on us to steal our
breath. Quit chasing me!

An Ocean Apart

"Sometimes she calls your brother Fernando my brother's name, Juan José," my mom had warned me. The ground shifted under my feet.

Last week of a cold December in Almeria, and I braced myself for the sight of my ninety-seven-year-old great-aunt disoriented for the first time in her life. Her mind had always been as sharp as the pair of shears in her old sewing box. Only four months earlier, she could recite passages from Cervantes's *Don Quixote*, and Jorge Manrique's *Coplas on the Death of His Father*. I stumbled, almost fell on the floor.

The main room in her nursing home was lively with the voices of family members visiting their old relatives. Sitting next to a window, my aunt looked out at the people in a frenzy, buying presents for the Eve of Three Kings. When I called her, "Tita," she looked at me and said, "Mi rubia!" A smile slowly formed in her face. I regained my balance.

We spent hours holding hands in silence, knowing what we could not vocalize but her foggy eyes revealed, fixed in the afterlife, lost in the space between us. A barrier greater than the Sea of Atlas would soon separate us forever. My body was still as a glass of water.

Three weeks later, January 2008, I felt as if I was standing on the edge of a cliff at the news of her death: "It was peaceful; she left us while sleeping; I was holding her hands." My mom's words prompted an avalanche of pain from my head to my toes and even beyond, burying me alive. It was as if I were underwater.

Sitting in the backyard of my Houston house that evening, I looked at the sky, searching for her in the stars, wanting to see her again, shining and guiding me with her light. I wished we were just an ocean apart. I closed my eyes and cried till I ran out of tears, at a loss for how to survive this new drought.

Intruders

8AM
I'm driving on I-45 North to work—four lanes
packed with sleep-deprived commuters. A man with
     greying hair drinks
his Starbucks while checking the Houston traffic
on his GPS. A young brunette adds mascara to her
     already thick lashes
between stops. I turn up the radio and listen to the
     Roula and Ryan Show. The
Weeknd is on when an image flashes through my
     brain—

my brother   lying unconscious   inside his car, upside down
     like a tortoise   flipped onto its back.   His leather seat
                              soaked with blood.

Are you okay? I type in WhatsApp, my eyes moving
     fast
from road to phone back to road, till his words on the
     screen, *Yes,*
why? let go of the hand crushing my chest.

1PM

I open the door to my office. My classes went well.
	Students
talked, laughed, and left without questions. I check
	my phone. I
have one missed call—my son's school nurse. The
	message cuts
off after the first three words—*Hello, my name (blank).*
	Silence
follows and my head fills up with voices in panic:

something's wrong   jackson is sick   but he wasn't this morning
	maybe he fell another kid hit him what if he's hurt?
he needs you   why didn't you check your phone before?

I call the number, my heart in my ears. I
can hardly hear the nurse's request to bring
an updated record of my son's shots for the current
	year.

7PM

It's time to cook supper—cherigan mixto with melted
cheese and tuna using my mom's aioli recipe,
	the one I
wrote in a post-it note that I can't find now. It's 2AM
in Spain. Mom is asleep. Too late for a call.
	Then, it happens,
the kitchen vanishing and I am in my head, the voices
coming like party crashers—

	What will you do when your mom is gone?

41

Will you be able to tell her goodbye?
Will she leave knowing her life was worthy?
Who will tell you yours is, too?
Will home in Spain still be home?
How will you fill her absence?

Pain pours out my eyes, a torrent I can't swim against.

I can't stop them—the voices, the panic,
forcing themselves in until I
am forced out.

Who Can Answer?

I.

My seven-year-old son wears Adidas to school, his
books and supplies in his Roblox backpack. Side-
swept hair with short sides is his new style, while
another boy, a seven-year-old somewhere, wears a
hospital gown as his second skin, bald, not the thick
hair from before.

Tubes follow him wherever he goes.

II.

I sleep in a king-size bed, my neck supported by two
feathery pillows, my well-fed body covered by a silky
nightgown and a comforter, light as the AC-
controlled air of my bedroom, while a man in worn-
out clothes, two sticks as arms, his elbows sharp like
needles, uses a cardboard box as a mattress in a dark
alley.

Broadsheet newspaper pages are his only blanket.

III.

Why? Why do I have everything I need—even
        everything I don't—
                food, junk or gourmet, takeout or homemade,
                        it doesn't matter,
                a roof over my head, a mansion for many
                        people's standards,

a well-paid job, with health insurance and
        pension plans, and perks
                like summers off while being paid,
                        time I use to go to Spain,
a family, both nuclear and extended, all alive
        and healthy,
money to spend and waste on hobbies,
        clothes, shoes, toys,
                electronics, entertainment, travel, you
                name it?

Why? Why me and not others who instead are born
    in poverty, no home suitable for living, no food to
        grow healthy,
                no warmth to radiate more warmth,
    of violence, domestic, external, or both,
    of broken households because of divorce,
        desertion, despair,
    of war, the toy in a kid's hands an assault rifle?

Who decides what is wrong or right? Could we
choose where, when, and how to be born? Could we
choose our genes, our looks, our health? How many
choices did we have at birth?

And why? Why do I feel I should burn in the depths
of hell for having everything and feeling empty, a well
full of frozen water?

I am thirsty.

Tic Toc, Tic Toc

In a race against
time, I lose. A fast runner,
I can't keep his pace.

Grading Hurts Like an Open Sore

It makes me shrink like a linen shirt
in the dryer. It itches like a bite
from a fire ant, the skin around red,
like a knee scratched against gravel,
with pus at the center, yellow-white,
hard, so hard I squeeze it to no avail.

Grading haunts me like the ghost
of a long-gone friend I betrayed
and never asked for forgiveness.
I take it everywhere—home, Starbucks,
the lake house—like my heart, which sinks
at the sight of failure, the sailboat swallowed
by a giant wave. Give me twenty papers,
and my legs want to run away though my feet
don't move from the ground. Give me eighty,
and my soul screams like a pig being slaughtered,
yet my eyes are trapped by the words.

I'm a bird in a cage and I surrender—though the wild
tiger in me roars to be free.

not yet no time

days are short
weeks fly by
i have to run
run to work
run from class
to class
run to school
to pick up
my son
run to the store
run, run, run
home
kids
work
come first
i
come last
back pain? pill.
sore throat? pill
no sleep? pill
pills that don't
slow life
stop! breathe!
i can't
not yet no time

In Need of a Magic Pill

> ". . . The pregnant heart
> is driven to hopes that are the wrong
> size for this world."
> ~Jack Gilbert, "Trouble." *Refusing Heaven*

Slowly, I drink my cup of milk with Nescafé,
not too cold, not too hot, just perfect to warm
up my stomach without upsetting it. Sitting
by the kitchen bar top this morning, the weight
of daily routine threatens to crush me like a crane
collapsing on a car in a construction site.

I need to wash the dishes from last night,
   vacuum the downstairs floor,
     make the beds,
       cook for lunch,
        take a shower,
          sit in front of my laptop,
            plan lessons for my next class.

I'll be interrupted by my son's need of a snack,
e-mails demanding a prompt answer, online training
   sessions
here and there on how to be accessible, engaging,
nurturing to my students so that they don't give up.

I eat lunch,
                    wash the dishes,
                                work some more
till my son needs another snack, supper, and attention
that I can hardly give him, for which I feel badly.

The what-to-do list increases
        when I must go to the store,
            or the bank,
                    and wash, dry, and fold clothes,
                    and put them away,
                    and grade papers,
                            and offer my students feedback in
                                a loving way that promotes
                                growth, not disappointment.

When it is time for bed, I know that the next day
will be the refrain for this constant song of my life.

So I wonder, what's the point? The kitchen
never stays clean for long, the dogs always
bring dirt and mud from outside, we need
to eat several times a day, so food needs to be
cooked and bought with money from the bank
that I need to earn by teaching students whose
hearts and minds I want to touch but sometimes
I can't, students who want to find a good job so
that they can earn money . . . and what's the point?

To earn that money, they will have to work long
hours, like me, hours that they won't have to
spend time with their sons, whom they'll teach
to continue the cycle of life without living, until
they are old, or sick, or they die.

"So tell me, what is the point of life?" I ask
my husband, while I take sips of my warm cup
of milk with Nescafé, looking for an answer
that can lift the heavy crane from my crushed
heart. "I think you need to ask your doctor
to change your treatment," he answers, looking
at me with concerned eyes, while I wish there
was a pill, a magic pill, that could show me
the answer to the meaning of my life.

II
DROWNING

I Feel Like . . .

A cheap piece
of false gold—

Old Slemmons in
"The Gilded Six-Bits"—

a bumper sticker
on a Ferrari,

a soured preacher
without a sermon,

a five-year-old kid
hiding in her closet,

waiting to be
rescued

from herself.

Days of Blue

Sometimes, life is a hundred-pound backpack
that you must carry on your shoulders every day.
        You just can't stand, even less move. Life
        is too heavy, so hard you cannot carry its
                weight.
        Your body aches; your bones will crack until
                they break.

Other times, life is a five-thousand-piece puzzle,
each piece the same color as most of the others.
        You cannot put the pieces together. Life
        is confusing, too difficult to view the whole
        with its parts. Some are missing; others do not
                match.

Or maybe I'm just too weak or ready to give up.

The Depression Test

Choose the image that best represents your state of
    mind:

1.
A dense black veil spreads
over the sky. Its blackness
blinds you to the sun.

2.
Clouds gather in grief.
The sun is wrapped in a black
shroud for burial.

The Soul Killer

I have a demon in my mind.
He never seems to sleep and likes
creeping through my head to my eyes
where he sits, obstructing my view,

and he becomes the only sight
I have. A demon in my mind
glares down at me with blood-red eyes,
freezing up my veins till my legs

refuse to walk; my skin can't feel
the warmth of hands. Beware! Inside
I have a demon. In my mind,
no room is left for play or laughs,

just him, trampling on my senses.
I've become a walking shadow
reflecting his crippling power.
I have a demon in my mind.

The Fall

Standing against the wall of my past, no visible path
    to a future ahead.

To my right
the blazing sun
on the bare shoulders
of little kids,
whooping at play
with delta kites,
painting the sky
with downward strokes,
whipped by the strength
of howling winds.

To my left
a deep pit
made of stone,
with jagged edges
and mossy walls
humming the tunes
of those who lost
the sight of the sun,
of playful kids,
of dancing kites
propelled by the wind
whipping the sky.

I look down
the pit,
stumble
and fall,
hitting
      the walls
           of no__
                thing__
                    ness__

When You Stop Caring

I don't want morning to come. I don't want to open
my eyes. I don't want to see sunlight stream through
the slats, announcing the beginning as if nothing. So
I lie down in bed, a moth in a spider web. Darkness
helps me forget I should fight. Sadness brings silence,
no voices screaming, demanding, demeaning, a silence
swaddling me for sleep.

The phone rings and rings, till it stops. It rings and
    rings
again. It stops. My husband is worried. How hard it
    must
be to see me break apart time and again. Tears form a
    blue
ring on the pillow, here, in the dark woods.

A few minutes later—maybe hours—he rushes into
    our bedroom,
pulls back the curtains, opens the blinds, and grabs
    me in his arms.
"We are going to the doctor's office," he says,
    without expecting
a reply. With my arms around his neck and my head
    on his shoulder,
he carries the dead weight of my body, lifting the
    heavy burden
of someone who has stopped caring.

In Answer to Those Who Say the Voices in My Head Are Not Real

I hear a mob of angry people yelling,
a demolition on a construction site. I
don't know what they want—the voices.
I just want silence, no more jackhammers
cracking the pavement of my brain.

I see the voices in the woman in the mirror: in her
hazel irises when they turn greener inside
and darker around their edge, bloodshot eyes—
lids too heavy and waterlogged to remain open;
in her body—her sharp shoulder blades, jutting
clavicles, the marked outline of her sternum,
spine, twenty-four ribs, and hip bones; in her
skin, the color of bleached bones, thin as the peel
of a yellow plum.

The voices taste like milk that has gone
bad, and soon enough the sourness is
in my stomach. Sweet treats are
never sweet; I feel the voices' bile
morning, evening, night,
awake and asleep.

I can smell the voices in the greasy strands
of hair whirl-pooling in the tub, in the dirty
clothes falling out of the hamper, in the weeks-
old food in the refrigerator—the moldy broccoli,
the spoiled apples, the rotten beef.

The voices have sharp edges. They hurt
my hands when I try to write down
the pain they cause—the brick block
in my chest rubbing up and down
against my sternum, stopping the air
to my lungs, the cold sweat bringing
shivers down my spine, the cramps
in my legs, the tightness in my neck,
the weight on my back that bends me
down until I only want to lie down
and sleep forever so that I stop hearing
the voices in my head.

In the Midst of Battle

I never wanted this war with my brain,
the powerful general that commands
my memories, my thoughts, my feelings.

I never asked for a fight, the smoking
cannons, fire consuming flesh, burning
bones, horses tossed into the mud.
Besides, I love peace, the peace
that comes with the caress of the waves
against the shore, or the clouds' white
strokes on the blue-sky canvas.

It is not easy to pull away from its arms,
which squeeze my heart so hard
that not enough blood runs
into my lungs, bending me
down while I'm gasping.

I beg it to stop, on my knees,
crying like a baby just pushed
out of her mother's womb.

Yet, my brain is a tyrant,
breaking down my resistance,
waiting for me to stop breathing.

Suicide Note

Dear All,

I'm tired of wanting to breathe
in a world with not enough air
to fill my shriveled lungs.

I'm tired of the iron ball,
stuck in my throat,
that gives me two choices:
gag or keep my mouth shut.

I'm tired of the light outside
that burns my eyes as I try
to look away from the screaming voices
trapped inside my mind.

I'm tired of feeling guilty
for failing to be thankful
and happy for what I have,
and I don't give a damn.

I'm tired of the emptiness that inhabits
each cell of my body,
usurping
all the blood in my veins.

I am tired of letting
you down, unable to be
the kind of person
you wish I was.

 "Cheer up, mujer!" you say,
"your sadness makes no sense,"
but it is only my sadness
that I sense.

Sorry if I hurt
you once again,
but rest assured this
will be the last time
I'll cause you any pain.

III
SWIMMING

In the Therapist's Chair
(on how to cope with repressed anger)

    I.

When I am angry, I cry.   Why?
I don't know. It makes me sad,   I guess.
I should scream instead,   right?
But I don't,   until I do,   and then,
the earth cracks open and swallows me
    and those I'm angry at.
So instead, I stay quiet and sad,
and my thoughts overfeed my stomach, my mind,
and I can't eat or sleep,   only think . . .

. . . think of the times growing up when I was
    drowning in the challenging waters of my father's
    "everything you do, you have to do it right,"

. . . or the day in the car when I was playing 'N Sync,
    and Migue changed stations saying what I
    listened to was trash.

. . . think of the times I told Doug not to call me after
    he broke up, cause it hurt too much, but he
    called and called, until I gave up and picked up
    the phone,

. . . or the night I pretended to like beer so that David
        didn't think I was weird. I ended up on one of
        the pub tables passed out, with ice on my neck
        until I woke up.

Thoughts fill me up and I want to vomit
them, but they stay inside and more come.
I overflow and there is nothing but streams of anger,
of pain, of regret, of self-pity, pouring out of my eyes.

II.

*If you are angry because you are not given the respect you
                                deserve, speak up! Complain!
Define your own boundaries and don't let others cross them
                                without your permission.*

*Act of your own volition and don't blame yourself for wanting
                                to live your life. That is your right,
Whenever you're angry and feel overflown, let anger appear and
                                give her a voice.*

*She needs to be heard. Be clear. Express her in words,
                                not tears.*

The Winter Waves

breathe gusts of angry
winds out. Appeased, foamy hands
stroke my swollen feet.

The Naked Child

She hides in the crammed attic of my childhood
memories, behind the wooden dresser
with white drawers and orange knobs
where I kept my collection of conch shells –
those filled with ocean whispers crashing
against the silence of my bedroom
on Sunday evenings.

Longing to be found, she sits on the cold
floor curled up; her glassy eyes scream
in the darkness, a cloak around her nine-
year-old body. Yet, no tears run down
her cheeks, no sobs escape her lips,
subdued by layer upon layer of neglect.

I've paid for my negligence, though.
I've cried her thwarted tears,
I've shaken with her choked-back sobs.
I've been a puppet of a girl puppeteer
tangled in strings she cannot control.

She pulls; I hang;
She yanks; I yank back
'till sore and breathless,
we stop, sitting on the cold floor
curled up, behind the old wooden dresser
with white drawers and orange knobs.
We meet each other's eyes, glassy eyes,
whose voice will be hushed no more.

A Poetic Reminder to My Forgetful Self

I am . . .

not the wide and sturdy lifeboat
that can take stranded travelers away
from the wreckage of their lives;

not the glue
that can piece back together
a shattered crystal glass of dreams;

not the antidote
for the fever of apathy and the poison of habit
that kill the most determined will;

but the river that grows darker
as toxic sewage is dumped
on its banks,

and the river that swells after
months of steady downpours
'till it floods.

A Foggy Morning Lesson

A thick fog curtain
falls between cars and the road.
Eyes can't see yonder.

Group Therapy Discovery Machine

Today is our weekly Thursday meeting. We sit on the
    floor, two
yoga cushions for each of the twelve of us, lost souls
    in search

of a place to fit in this world. In the room, though,
    we all know our spots:
mine between Rafa, the browless twenty-year-old with
    uneven stubble,

and María, addicted to meth (and a controlling
mother she can't live with or without).

Me? I just want to learn how to stop others from
    stepping
on my toes before they are bruised, bleeding, and I
    can't walk.

Today, we must build a machine together. "Stand up
    and place
yourselves where you think the part you represent

should be." Jesús and Dolores set a timer for two
    minutes and observe:

Rafa, the first to go,
chooses engine. He sits
on the floor, legs crossed
and arms around his waist.
María, steering wheel, stands
behind Rafa, her hands holding
the air in front of her chest.
Rocío becomes the trunk, hands
and knees on the floor like a cat
yoga pose.

Teresa and Tomás are tires;   they form a ball with
their bodies.

Brakes, battery, alternator, AC compressor, muffler,
radiator complete the machine (except for me).

Time ticktocks. What could I be? (*hurryhurry*).
Something
different (*thinkthink*), something special (*hurryhurry*),
a you'll-never-forget-

this-machine-part something. I stand tall
with open arms to the right. I am *the* ultimate

decoration, the only light-up ornament in an old
Christmas tree,
the vanilla-cinnamon added flavor in plain hot milk.
Jesús asks

us to own our place, feel its weight in our bodies,
    its effect
on other parts, while Dolores circles around,
    watching us.

It begins in my feet,
        goes up through my spine
            until it reaches my head, the force

of a vacuum sucking
        all happy particles from my body.

My previous smile fades like a sunflower head
    drooping
            at the passing of a storm cloud.

Eleven people surround me. I am
            nothing
            but a hole on the ground:

depthless,   dark,   desolate.

How to Tame Wild Thoughts

Your mind knows no breaks. It works
when you read, when you write, when you teach,
       when you drive, when you walk, when you fly,
when you cook, when you clean, when you shower,
       when you watch TV, when you talk. Even when
       you sleep, it jerks you up, makes you scream, cry,
       kick, and punch the air.

Your mind never pauses. You are told, "Stop
       thinking,"
as if you could turn off your thoughts with a remote.
       You
can learn how to tame them, though, these wild
creatures. They like roaming over your body to find
extra space and avoid trampling on each other.
       Sometimes
they sit at the base of your skull till your head
       becomes too
heavy. Other times, they dwell in the pit of your
       stomach
and leave no room for food. If they sneak to your
       lungs, they
steal part of your air; if they anchor in your back, your
       spine creaks
and bends. They always make sure you know where
       they are.

So draw and do puzzles
                        to quiet your mind,
dance
        to shake the weight of your thoughts on your
                body, and

        turn your fidget spinner around and around

    thrown against a ceiling fan.   till its whirring sound

    them away like balloons   lulls them to sleep and
                                            sends

Weeds

I grow everywhere,
in fields, lawns, parks, vacant lots,
in flower beds, beside roadways,
even in places as small
as the gaps in the concrete of your driveway,
pushing up through the gravel.

You don't like me. I upset
the order you carefully work
on maintaining.

You see me as wild,
cumbering the ground
you believe you own
and have a right to control.

You see me as ugly,
hindering a beautiful form of life
from unfolding and flourishing.

You spray, cut, pull.
But you can't kill me.

I grow back.
I grow stronger,
and under the vast sky,
join the breeze in a dance
with many others who, like me,
may be wild and ugly,
but free.

The Wisdom of the Waves

They march on,
                    propelled by the wind and the moon.

No time to look back,
                    no room for thoughts of withdrawing.

They follow each other,
        in sync with the pace and needs
                            of their fellow travelers.

        If one slows down
a white foamy hand reaches out from behind
                    steering her by her shoulder.

If she is overcome with exhaustion
                    both merge and together,
                        they put on a show of
        strength.

Nothing can detain them:
                    no rocks, logs, or ragged shores.
                        They bend corners and climb up walls.

They become high jumpers
            turning in the air, curving their backs,
                        leaving barriers behind.

Flexible contortionists,
            they squeeze through the tiniest openings.

They march on,
            soaking up every second of their adventure.

Weird – Part II

"Why fit in, when you were born to stand out?"
~Dr. Seuss

Albert Einstein didn't like wearing
    socks.
He always got holes in them

                        Whimsical

Stephen Hawkins and his family
    spent
dinner time in silence reading books

                        Extraordinary

Harriet Tubman went into sleeping
spells with religious visions that guided
    her to help slaves escape

                        Inspiring

Emily Dickinson never married or had
children during a time when that was
    the norm for women

                        Rebellious

Wolfgang Amadeus Mozart wrote half
of the number of his symphonies
    between the ages of eight and nineteen

                        Dazzling

Undressing Darkness

Mourning clouds cover
the sky. Rain-like hands undress
my pollen-clad car.

Fuguilla[4]

A shooting star crosses the autumn sky—
dense clouds awaken from a long slumber;
they break a bit, and a solitary star appears—
shining bright, like a Harlem diva
behind the velvety red curtains
of the Apollo Theater.

Suddenly, there you are,
standing next to me in the kitchen
of Mom's house on a Saturday evening.
You're preparing gachas—your nail tips black
from peeling the charred skin
of roasted green peppers—stirring
the caldo de pimentón until it boils.
I'm washing dishes, cleaning the countertop
you covered in flour to knead the dough.
You take your time. I'm fast,
a "fuguilla," you say—your skin
wrinkled but soft, like a baby's,
to the touch. I smile.

---

[4] A person who moves and does everything fast, like a shooting star

It's been more years than I would like.
I look up to the sky, at the steady, solitary star.
It blinks at me.
I'm still a "fuguilla," tita;
you're still taking your time.

Self-Portrait as My Mother

Querida mamá:

The day last summer when you cried all the way
back from Exfiliana to Almería, muffling your sobs
with a package of Kleenex in the front seat of my
    rental
car, your silence spoke to me in words I could touch,
    words
that rubbed my heart, scratched my throat and made
    me bleed
inside, blood of your blood, causing pain of your
    pain. So I
talked for you and your words became mine. It hurts
    to feel
broken when others see you whole. Who will help fix
    you if
they see nothing wrong? It hurts to be older and feel
    like you
want to crawl back into your mother's womb. It hurts
    to hurt
the ones you love. Ahora lo sé, mamá, and because
    you knew
how much, you understood my silence the first time
    my words
failed me. It was the end of summer. I was only
    twenty-three,
sitting on the living-room couch, tissue in my hands,
    tears

down my cheeks, not a single sound coming from my
    mouth. I
stared at the air, thick with nothing. You held my
    hands, pulled me
up and said, "It's okay, mi cielo; we'll get some help."
    Twenty-three
years later, it was my turn to hold your hands and tell
    you, "It's
okay, mami; I'm here. I understand. We'll get some
    help."

Swimming, Not Drowning

I taught myself how to swim in the pool
of my family's duplex in Retamar.

I was ten, and I removed
my floaties, held the highest step

of the ladder in the deep end of the pool
and kicked my feet as fast as I could,

under my dad's watchful gaze.
I practiced for months 'till I could

let go of the step that helped me stay afloat
without sinking. How very proud I was

that day! In no time, I was swimming
the length of the pool from one end to the other

with no breaks to catch my breath
and no fear of drowning. The sea?

That was a different creature with life
of its own, sometimes tame, other times wild,

sometimes welcoming, others hostile,
always unpredictable. There was no ladder,

no edge I could hold on to if tired or scared. Windy
        days
were the worst. Poniente's large-capacity lungs

could blow up to six-foot waves. Those days
I stayed at the shore, keeping my distance

from the roaring sea rising and falling,
threatening to swallow me whole. Those days

I wondered what would take for me to join that
        energy,
that impetus of the sea, which hours later

became appeased, an infinite pond of clear water.
        Once,
days passed and the winds didn't cease. In my dreams,

I heard them whistle my name. They wanted me to
        swim
under the waves and emerge on the other side, where
        it's calm

and the sun sprinkles stardust on the surface of the
        sea
that bubbles up with excitement. They wanted me to
        know

I could swim the turbulent waters
                                    without drowning.

ABOUT THE AUTHOR

Mari-Carmen Marín was born in Málaga, on the southern Mediterranean coast of Spain, but moved to Houston, Texas, in 2003 after receiving her Ph.D. in African American literature from the University of Zaragoza (Spain). An avid reader and lover of literature from an early age, she began to write poetry to give a specific shape to, and be able to order, the chaotic and complex feelings and ideas running rampant in her mind. Writing poetry has become her comfy chair in front of a fireplace on a stormy winter day.

She prepared for a new career in poetry through online courses from Stanford Continuing Studies and attendance at many poetry workshops under the supervision of poets like Dave Parsons, Tony Hoagland, Courtney Kampa, Kirstin Andersen, Mong-Lan, and Beth Lyons. Her poems have appeared in several places, including, *Wordriver Literary Review*, *Scarlet Leaf Review*, *Dash Literary Journal*, *Months to Years*, *The Awakenings Review*, *Lucky Jefferson*, San Fedele Press, Willowdown Books, *The Comstock Review*, *The Green Light Literary Journal*, *Mothers Always Write*, *Breath & Shadow*,

The Ekphrastic Review, *Poets' Choice*, *Kaleidoscope*, *Toho Journal*, and *Poetica Review*. She currently works as a professor of English at Lone Star College at Tomball, Texas.

When she was younger, she dreamed about going to the United States some day, where she could begin a new life, teaching, writing, and making a difference in others' lives. It took her thirty years to figure out how to achieve her dream, but she has been living it for sixteen years now and counting.

62448562R00059